W9-CCC-618

HORSES

The Belgian Horse

by Sarah Maass

Consultant:
Staff of the Belgian Draft Horse
Corporation of America
Wabash, Indiana

Capstone
press

Mankato, Minnesota

Edge Books are published by Capstone Press,
151 Good Counsel Drive, P.O. Box 669, Mankato, Minnesota 56002.
www.capstonepress.com

Library of Congress Cataloging-in-Publication Data
Maass, Sarah.
    The Belgian horse / by Sarah Maass.
    p. cm.—(Edge Books. Horses)
    Summary: "Describes the Belgian horse, including its history, physical
features, and uses today"—Provided by publisher.
    Includes bibliographical references and index.
    ISBN 0-7368-4373-6 (hardcover)
    1. Belgian draft horse—Juvenile literature. I. Title. II. Series.
SF293.B4M24 2006
636.1'5—dc22   2004030226

Editorial Credits
Carrie A. Braulick, editor; Juliette Peters, designer; Deirdre Barton, photo
    editor/photo researcher

Photo Credits
Capstone Press/Gary Sundermeyer, 6, 9, 26
Cecil Darnell, back cover, 7, 8, 19, 20, 22
Cheval Photography, 12, 25
Karen Patterson, 5
Lynn M. Stone, 14
Mane Photo, cover
© Mark J. Barrett, 11, 16–17, 29
Photo of Captain Jim: Photo by the Draft Horse Journal, ©2003, 15
Photo of the Forty: Photo courtesy of the Draft Horse Journal, 27

1 2 3 4 5 6 10 09 08 07 06 05

Table of Contents

Chapter 1: Ancient Ancestors 4

Chapter 2: A Gentle Breed 10

Chapter 3: Powerful Pullers.................. 18

Chapter 4: Belgians in Action 24

FEATURES

Photo Diagram 16

Fast Facts... 28

Glossary 30

Read More 31

Internet Sites.. 31

Index... 32

Ancient Ancestors

About 1,000 years ago, knights in Europe rode horses into battle. Knights wore heavy metal armor to protect themselves. They needed strong horses to carry the extra weight of the armor. Flemish horses were the most common warhorses. Europeans called them "great horses" because they were tall and strong.

Belgian horses are descendants of Flemish horses. Many features that made Flemish horses popular also are found in Belgians.

Learn about:
★ **Flemish horses**
★ **Belgians on farms**
★ **A registry for Belgians**

Today's Belgians have large, muscular bodies like their ancestors did.

From War to Work

Flemish horses were popular warhorses throughout the Middle Ages (400–1500). Horse breeders in the European country of Belgium produced some of the best Flemish horses.

By the 1600s, smaller, faster horses had taken the place of Flemish horses in wars. Yet many horse breeders in an area of Belgium called Brabant kept breeding Flemish horses. Some people began calling these horses "Brabants." Europeans used Brabants and other draft horses for farmwork. Draft horses were first bred for work purposes instead of for riding. They are large and strong.

Developing the Belgian

People brought Brabants to the United States in the late 1860s. They became popular workhorses. Some Brabants pulled logs out of forests to clear land for homes and crops.

Long hair covers
the lower legs
of Brabants.

Until the early 1940s, many Belgians worked in fields.

In the late 1880s, some horse breeders in the United States wanted Brabants to be more stylish. Over time, these breeders produced horses that were less bulky than the European Brabants. Their horses also had less long hair, or feather, on their lower legs. People called these horses Belgians.

A Belgian Registry

In 1887, Belgian owners in the United States formed the American Association for the Belgian Horse. People registered their Belgians with the organization. The group then kept track of each registered horse's ancestry. Later, this registry's name changed to the Belgian Draft Horse Corporation of America.

Decline and a Comeback

In the early 1940s, many people began using tractors for farmwork. Tractors traveled faster than Belgians and other draft horses. Many people stopped breeding draft horses.

Belgians made a comeback in the late 1960s. This time, most people raised Belgians as a hobby instead of for farmwork. Some people competed with their Belgians at shows.

Today, more Belgians live in the United States than all other draft horse breeds combined. The Belgian Draft Horse Corporation of America has about 180,000 registered Belgians.

Chapter 2

A Gentle Breed

Belgians have large, powerful bodies to help them pull heavy loads. They have gentle, willing personalities. These qualities help make Belgians popular.

Size and Build

Horses are measured in hands. A hand equals 4 inches (10 centimeters). Belgians usually stand between 16 and 18 hands tall at the top of the shoulders, or withers. Many other horses stand only about 15 hands tall.

Belgians usually weigh between 1,800 and 2,000 pounds (800 and 900 kilograms). Some Belgian stallions weigh as much as 2,400 pounds (1,100 kilograms).

Learn about:
★ Size
★ Breed features
★ Colors and markings

10

Belgians have wide chests and thick, muscular legs.

Chestnut Belgians are a dark red-brown color.

Like other draft horses, Belgians are large and strong. They have wide chests and heavily muscled, sloping shoulders. They have short, wide backs and muscular hindquarters. Belgians have shorter legs and less feather than some other draft horse breeds.

Color

Many of the first Belgians in the United States were dark brown with black manes and tails. But most of today's Belgians have light blonde manes and tails with chestnut, sorrel, or blonde coats. All of these coat colors are red-brown. Chestnut is the darkest. Blonde is the lightest. Some Belgians are roan. These horses have a mixture of white hairs in their coats.

A blaze often reaches from the forehead to the nose.

Belgians often have white markings on their faces and legs. Some Belgians have a large white stripe on their face called a blaze. White markings on the lower legs include socks and stockings.

Personality

Belgians are known as the gentlest of all draft horses. Their patient, calm personalities have earned them the nickname "gentle giants."

Belgians are willing workers. Many Belgian owners say their horses seem to be happiest when they have a job to do.

McIlrath's Captain Jim

On February 20, 2003, a 2-year-old Belgian stallion named McIlrath's Captain Jim broke a world record. He was sold at the Mid-America Draft Horse Sale in Illinois for $112,500. No draft horse had ever sold for such a large amount of money. The old record sale price for a draft horse had been $47,000.

At the sale, Captain Jim attracted the attention of many Belgian breeders. These breeders believed that Captain Jim had many outstanding features that could be passed on to his offspring. James Raber and Orla Yoder of Topeka, Indiana, now own Captain Jim.

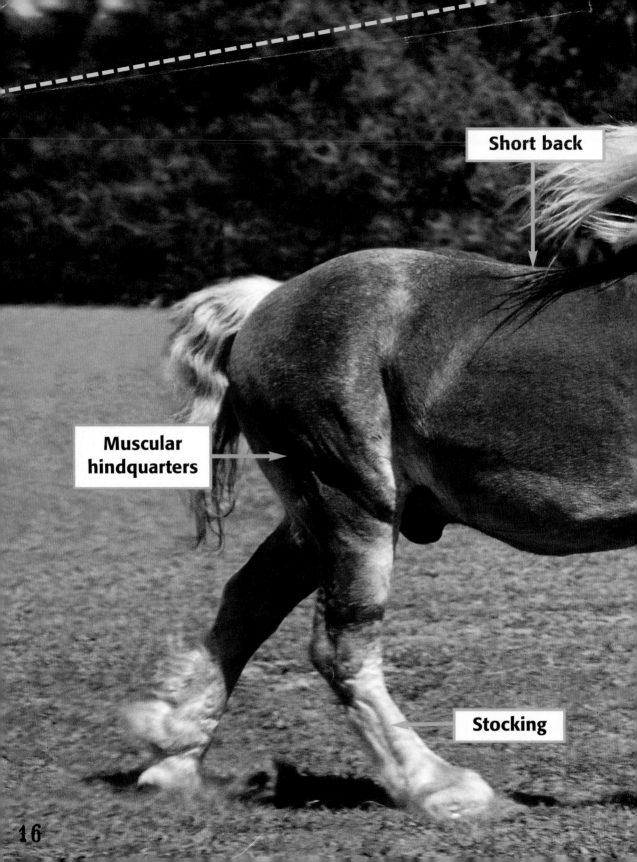

Short back

Muscular hindquarters

Stocking

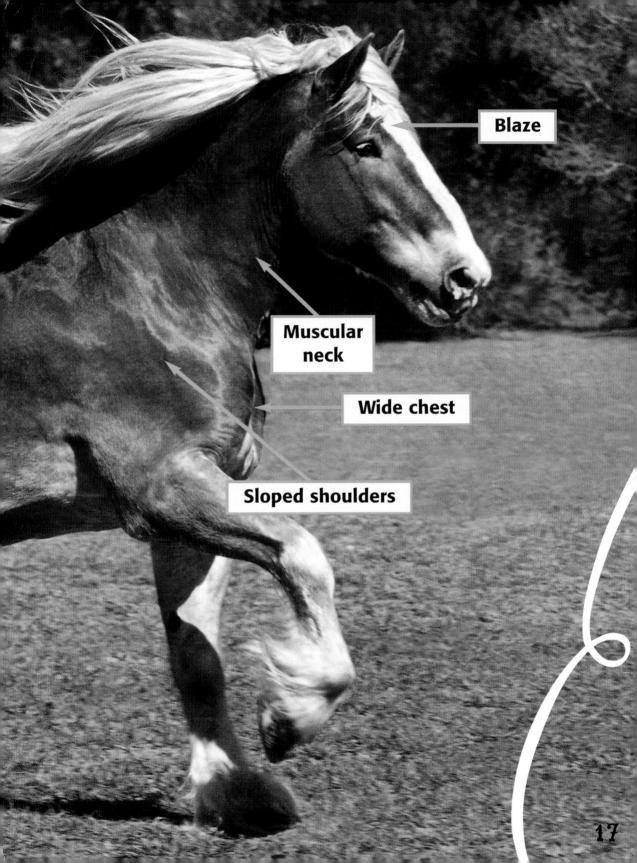

Blaze

Muscular neck

Wide chest

Sloped shoulders

Chapter 3

Powerful Pullers

In the late 1800s, farmers were proud of how much their horses could pull. They competed to see whose horses could pull the heaviest loads. Pulling competitions continued after tractors took the place of horses on farms.

Today, horsepulling is a popular sport throughout the world. Almost all horses in pulling competitions are Belgians. The horses have sturdy bodies that seem built to pull heavy loads.

Learn about:
- ★ **History of horsepulling**
- ★ **Contest rules**
- ★ **Training**

Belgians keep their willing attitudes even as loads get harder for them to pull.

Belgians pull loads a certain distance in pulling competitions.

Horsepulling Contests

In the United States, most horsepulling contests are in midwestern and eastern states. Many contests are held during county fairs. Each year, the World Championship Horse Pull is held during the Wayne County Fair in Michigan.

Participants in horsepulling contests follow a set of rules. Most contests give a team of two horses three tries to pull a load a certain distance. In eastern states, horses pull the load 6 or 12 feet (1.8 or 3.7 meters). In midwestern states, horses pull the load 27.5 feet (8.4 meters). Horses have five minutes to finish the pull. If they succeed, they try to pull a heavier load. The loads often weigh at least 2,000 pounds (900 kilograms).

Training Belgians to Pull

Two-year-old Belgians usually are ready to begin pulling carts. First, horses become used to wearing a harness and a bridle. The harness connects the horse to the cart. The bridle holds a metal piece in the horse's mouth. This piece is called a bit. Long straps called reins attach

Fieldwork can help keep Belgians fit.

Voice Commands

Voice commands help trainers guide their harness horses. The command to make the horses start moving is "giddyap." The command for stop is "whoa." Trainers say, "haw" for a left turn. For a right turn, the command is "gee."

to the bit. Trainers use the reins to turn and control the horse.

At first, trainers usually walk behind the horse and hold the reins. The horse learns to respond to voice commands and pressure from the bit. Later, trainers connect the horse to a cart.

Belgians continue growing until they reach about age 4. They then are ready to begin training for pulling contests. Trainers gradually build up their horses' strength for pulling contests. At first, the horses pull lightweight loads. Later, they pull heavier loads. Trainers may give their horses extra feed, vitamins, and minerals to keep them fit.

Chapter 4

Belgians in Action

Belgians are useful for many activities. A few people still use Belgians for farmwork. Other people use them to pull logs from forests. Belgians also are popular show and parade horses.

In the Show Ring

Belgians compete in draft horse shows throughout the United States. Show events include riding, halter, and hitch classes. In halter classes, handlers lead their horses. Judges score the horses on their physical features and movement. Horses pull carts in hitch classes.

Learn about:
★ Show classes
★ Caring for Belgians
★ A 40-horse hitch of Belgians

Some people ride Belgians in English riding classes at shows.

In 1988, draft horse owners started the North American Six-Horse Hitch Classic Series. Fifty shows throughout North America hold events for the series. Winning horses at these shows compete in the championship show. Thousands of people attend the championship each year.

Care

Caring for a Belgian is different from caring for a smaller horse. Belgians eat more than smaller horses do. Belgian owners also must supply their horses with larger stalls and exercise spaces.

Belgians are good all-around draft horses. People can train Belgians for almost any job. Their many abilities help make them America's most popular draft horses.

A 40-Horse Belgian Hitch

Large teams of Belgians often pull wagons in parades. In 1972, Dick Sparrow hitched a 40-horse team of Belgians together. The team was a re-creation of the famous Barnum and Bailey Circus parade horses from the early 1900s. Sparrow's hitch first appeared in the Schlitz Circus Parade in Milwaukee, Wisconsin. Until 1977, his hitch was the center of attention in many parades throughout the United States.

Sparrow's sons, Paul and Robert, put together another 40-horse hitch in 1989. This hitch appeared in Milwaukee's Great Circus Parade until 2002.

Fast Facts:
The Belgian Horse

History: Horse breeders in Belgium bred Brabants in the 1600s. In the 1860s, people brought Brabants to the United States. Horse breeders in the United States bred Brabants to create the modern Belgian.

Height: Belgians usually stand between 16 and 18 hands (about 6 feet or 1.8 meters) tall at the withers. Each hand equals 4 inches (10 centimeters).

Weight: 1,800 to 2,000 pounds (800 to 900 kilograms)

Colors: chestnut, sorrel, blonde, roan

Features: short, wide back; muscular hindquarters; wide chest; sloped shoulders; muscular neck

Personality: gentle, cooperative, calm

Abilities: Many Belgians compete in pulling competitions. Belgians also are popular show and parade horses.

Life span: about 20 years

Glossary

ancestor (AN-sess-tur)—a member of a breed that lived a long time ago

armor (AR-mur)—a protective metal covering

bit (BIT)—the metal mouthpiece of the bridle

bridle (BRYE-duhl)—the straps that fit around a horse's head and connect to a bit to control a horse while riding and driving

feather (FETH-ur)—long hair on the lower legs of some draft horses

harness (HAR-niss)—a set of leather straps and metal pieces that connect a horse to a plow, cart, or wagon

knight (NITE)—a warrior who fought on horseback in the Middle Ages

registry (REH-juh-stree)—an organization that keeps track of the ancestry for horses of a certain breed

stallion (STAL-yuhn)—an adult male horse that can be used for breeding

withers (WITH-urs)—the top of a horse's shoulders

Read More

Dalgleish, Sharon. *Working Horses.* Farm Animals. Philadelphia: Chelsea House, 2005.

Hull, Mary E. *The Horse in Harness.* The Horse Library. Philadelphia: Chelsea House, 2002.

Ransford, Sandy. *Horse and Pony Breeds.* Kingfisher Riding Club. Boston: Kingfisher, 2003.

Internet Sites

FactHound offers a safe, fun way to find Internet sites related to this book. All of the sites on FactHound have been researched by our staff.

Here's how:

1. Visit *www.facthound.com*
2. Type in this special code **0736843736** for age-appropriate sites. Or enter a search word related to this book for a more general search.
3. Click on the **Fetch It** button.

FactHound will fetch the best sites for you!

Index

appearance, 8, 10, 13, 14
    colors, 13
    markings, 14

Belgian Draft Horse Corporation
    of America, 9
bits, 22, 23
Brabants, 6, 8
bridles, 22

care, 26

feather, 8, 13
Flemish horses, 4, 6, 7

harnesses, 21, 22
horse shows, 9, 24, 26
    North American Six-Horse
      Hitch Classic Series, 26

knights, 4, 7

McIlrath's Captain Jim, 15

parades, 24, 27
personality, 10, 14
pulling competitions, 18, 21, 23
    rules, 21
    training for, 23
    World Championship Horse
      Pull, 21

reins, 22–23

size, 10, 13

training, 22–23